Human Crying Daisies

Human Crying Daisies

prose poems

Ray Gonzalez

Red Hen Press 🐔 Los Angeles

Cover collage by Christine Boyka Kluge
Front cover layout by Thea Kluge

Book design by Mark E. Cull

ISBN 1-888996-76-5
Library of Congress Catalog Card Number: 20031121322

The City of Los Angeles Cultural Affairs Department, California Arts Council and
the Los Angeles County Arts Commission partially supports Red Hen Press.

Red Hen Press
www.redhen.org

First Edition
Printed in Canada

ACKNOWLEDGMENTS

The author thanks the editors of these publications where the poems first appeared.

Alaska Quarterly Review: "Green Man"; *American Poetry Review*: "The Owl"; *Best American Poetry 2003*: "Max Jacob's Shoes"; *Bitter Oleander*: "Faith," "Listening to Santana," "Toca"; *Café Review*: "Cornudas," "Fetish," "Blind Animal Tracks," "Exhausted Notebook"; *Calapooya*: "Lesson"; *Carnegie Mellon Review*: "Sticky Monkey Flowers" "Black Winged Butterfly"; *Columbia*: "The Grape"; *Diagram*: "The Age"; *Electronic Poetry Review*: "Forever's Violin"; *Elixir*: "A Painting is Never in Love With Itself"; *Gargoyle*: "Bamboo Face"; *Green Mountains Review*: "Dropping Beads of Sweat on a Book by Robinson Jeffers"; *Heliotrope*: "What Color is Your Mexican?" "The Quest"; *Hotel Amerika*: "The Shiver"; *Indiana Review*: "The Blessing"; *Homestead Review*: "The Bat" "Forth" "Corn Face Mesilla" "Man With Blue Guitar"; *Kestrel*: "The Ginko Tree" "In Memorium" "History"; *Luna*: "Make a Little Star" "Twentieth Century Water"; *Many Mountains Moving*: "The Missing Arm of the Father"; *New American Writing*: "A.D." "After Ten Attempts" "Inscription" "He Calls His Dog Rimbaud" "Cadets at the Virginia Military Institute" "Masa Face" "Max Jacob's Shoes"; *New Orleans Review*: "And There Were Swallows"; *No Boundaries: Prose Poems by 24 American Poets* (Tupelo Press): "A Painting is Never in Love," "As If Talking," "Fucking Aztecs, Palomas, Mexico," "He Calls His Dog Rimbaud," "Joan Miro Threw a Stone at God," "The Bat," "The Black Torso of the Pharaoh," "The Blessing," "Traditional," and "Understanding."; *Pavement Saw*: "The Bleeding Foot"; *Ploughshares*: "Black Wasp"; *Portland Review*: "Media Monster Marries Mother"; *Red Rock Review*: "The Donkey Cart Apparition"; *Sentence*: "Coltrane";

Snow Monkey: "Snails" "Stung By a Beetle" "The Flash"; *The Drunken Boat:* "La Cueva Prehistoric Site, Organ Mountains, New Mexico"; *Witness:* "The White Squirrel"; *3rd Bed:* "Appearance Appetite" "The Mind Reader"; *6,500:* "Leaving the Last Century."

A special thanks goes to Yaddo, The Loft Studio Program, and The Pike's Peak Writer's Retreat for time and space to write many of these poems. For their belief in the prose poem and their years of support, I thank John Bradley, George Kalamaras, Morton Marcus, and Peter Johnson. For a lifetime of inspiration toward the prose poem, the light shines on Eduardo Galeano, Julio Cortázar, Max Jacob, Barry Yourgrau, Charles Simic, Russell Edson, and Robert Bly.

TABLE OF CONTENTS

Part One

Part Three

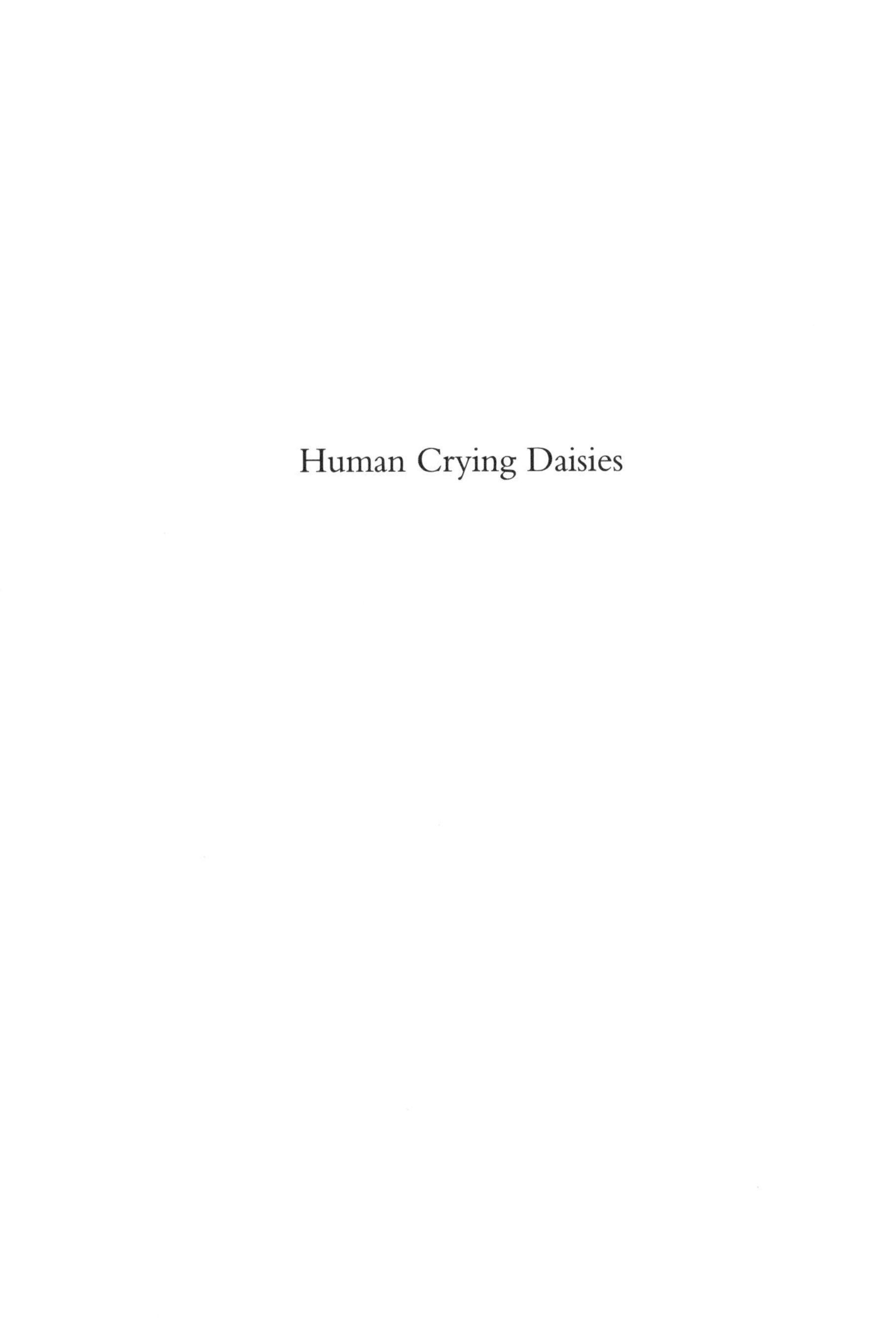

Human Crying Daisies

Part One

The necklace remains as the pet iguana lunges at the standing mirror when it sees itself. I was told to watch for the willow that resembles its tail, answer the face to see what it repeats of my beloved song. The fox crossed my path and looked back at me, its first appearance on my walk the last time I went that way—a pentagram handed off in the dark, on the pine cone a spot of blood, the frozen snail guiding the path. This world kissing the throne, someone wearing the beads, a voice nudging me awake. The old man moving his eyes in the painting, his chin getting warm without doves in flight. So the fox is red and disappears, burning permission granted. To touch its path with vowels. How strange to be seen under the cottonwood. This apple, the church without a forest, the wet night after I praise what I don't know, don't carry enough blame to silhouette my heart. In every broken necklace of love, the misspelled words.

The Part That Is Sacrificed

Belongs to the old way of thinking. I could stay here and find out why the ghost shattered my plate, how it moved by itself on the table, left my hands and scraped across the top before something tossed it against the wall. The part I don't believe, the thing that was sacrificed was how beautiful it was to know there was someone there. The presence had to leave me, go toward the closed eyes when what we know and what we are told have taken their gravity, flamed into one pink blossom gestating on the front porch, not a third thing nor the plunging stream of belief. The moisture to lean upon, open my eyes and see how I could have confronted it, gripped the plate tighter, my turn on the platform where the man in black stands waiting, his arms crossed on his chest, the white dish that flew from my hands spinning and hovering like a shield in front of his face.

One morning, my big toe hurt with the buried seed of the working man—my uncle I never knew who gave me his feet so I could walk away from the truth, sending him a message in an oversized shoe to encourage him to bring me a crimson robe—an ash for the forehead—his old army uniform and the sword with jagged edge where he cut off the Japanese head. One morning, I became a snowy yard—a cottonwood full of moss—a cicada changing sound—moldy bread on the ground—watermelon seeds—stinking rinds—a crazy flame from a village boy who burned down the only movie house in the town. I sat down to a fried egg, my grandmother frying it so I could quit crying and go play outside as soon as I could, the boys next door waiting to beat me up as I came out with a full stomach and a baseball bat.

He Calls His Dog Rimbaud

after Charles Simic

The sausages have been sliced. The wine has grown old. The piano notes belong to the man lifting his hands from brushing Rimbaud, his dog. Women have left him. One or two poems belong in the books. He has a gift for knowing what people will do. He was cited as the one who found the image hidden inside the caves of the emperor. When he writes, his dog howls and gives him ideas to take on the boat. The hat and boots have been laid out. The perfumed photo of the woman has been torn. The piano notes settle in the soul of the quiet man hugging his pet and asking for a growl. He will meet the light on the next continent, walk toward it because everyone wants him to explain why other dogs ran away from him. He is driven to get to the source of this dog. He must find why the paws trouble his sleep, why he has to leave in order to speak and try to imitate the dumb dog by barking at nothing in the street. He must find why the wagging tongue of the animal hangs so far out of its mouth, so he calls out to his dog, "Rimbaud! Come here, boy!"

In the sleep of disappearance, it hovered over the leaf as if I had been here before to hold out my hand and scare it away. In the stone tower across the lake, piano music invaded the death masks and turned them into disguises for the living who held their tongues over the water so the dragonfly could float there and touch them for an instant, the moment each person who survived the touching knew what the hurt was about. In the lake where it emerged, I saw the dragonfly one last time and waited for a day, weeks from now, when I could walk away without seeing my mother binding her hair to the lowest fern growing out of the water.

Make a Little Star
after Julio Cortazar

Make a little star by pulling a hair off your head and placing it in a glass jar. Heat the jar over the stove without concern for the reaction. After picking up the pieces of glass and throwing them away, step outside before the sun goes down. You will find the hair floating way off in the distant sky like the tail of a comet you were taught to identify. Make a little galaxy by pulling a second hair off your sweating head and dropping it on the ground. Don't bother to search for it. You will not find it because the earth is not gentle enough and will not allow you to take back your wishes. A child's hand will appear in the rhythm of your heart. You will know this when the little star begins to fall across the night sky. When you look up, this child will be a fresh constellation in everything you have desired. After naming this formation in your mind, do not share it or reveal the name. Keep it to yourself and the deep-rooted cause of your doubts will emerge when the shooting star is replaced by the scorpion tail you brought back from the desert in a sandwich bag, the body of the creature turning to dust on your mother's floor, the crushed geometry of its threat mapped out for you to think about. Make a little progress by pulling your hair one last time. When the short strands hurt and don't come out, stop what you are doing. The child's hand has quit waving goodbye.

When you visit me, bring the thing you love the most. Carry it in your heart and pretend the world will never end. When you visit me, recall a toy you had as a child, an object you forgot about quickly when someone bought you another. When you come, don't forget the passion in the bowl of fruit, the lovely pear sitting there waiting for the story of a train that appeared in a legend you were told at bedtime long ago. When you arrive, wait until the fire goes out and I can bring you grasshoppers from bitter cold regions, collections of stockings for fallen ankles, hummingbird images from a forest where many women have waited for me. When you visit me, be patient with the last thing you kissed, how the lips were warm and a trace of yearning fell in the mist. Don't worry about me having lost my ability to read. Your note is fresh on my mind and boats are waiting at the dock for one of us to appear.

Listening to Santana

after Juan Felipe Herrera

The guitar screamed and she came out from behind the flames. She was someone I knew in another life. She had no name and I had nothing to say. The guitar screamed and the men played cards before going upstairs to sound the alarm. They were angry, drunk, and revolutionaries of the quickest kind. The guitar slowed down and I kissed a fish. It must have been a fish because it fried like the meal we are given before we die. I told somebody I was going away. The mountains parted and I saw the canyon. When the guitar cut loose and the timbales crashed into vibrating wood, I was met by an angry crowd and elected prince. I ruled for two centuries, until they found me perfectly bound and preserved at the most popular tourist bar in Santa Fe. When his guitar shouted from atop the pyramid, I was taught by sound and the riot police. It was near the end of the song and I had seconds to pull the cottonwood tree out of my nose and plant it on the exact spot the first Spanish explorer would cross, his Walkman headphones muddy and twisted, the melting tape player auctioned to the crowd which was already burning the seats and asking for the horse, the rider, his armor—that tangle of guitar strings broken when the sun rose to pull the plug.

In the hour of the piano, I saw the ghost. In the hour of apprenticeship, I heard the ghost. In the hour of learning, I felt the ghost. In the hour of doubt, I smelled the ghost. In the hour of smoke, I could have burned the ghost. In the hour of commission, I paid the ghost. In the hour of things to come, I predicted the ghost. In the hour of light, I blinded the ghost. In the hour of black, I refused the ghost. In the hour of nutrition, I fed the ghost. In the hour of starvation, I was not enough for the ghost. In the hour of minutes, I aged with the ghost. In the hour of seconds, I passed the ghost. In the hour of the hour, the ghost passed through me.

Wombs belong to strangers that never loved me. Don't stop me. I can't spell the excitement trapped in the wall by the mural of the fish eaten by a naked man and woman who came here to save the tiny bones of the spine they carry between their bare toes. Against the moon is a dish of seeds I couldn't reach without lying to my mother, hating her when she censored photos of naked women in ads of the *LA Free Press* I subscribed to in high school, using her black crayon to hide what she didn't want me to see. It was dangerous to be influenced by the naked breast, the nipple, the surge and the lift with the eye focusing on what flesh spells what flesh bleeds what flesh becomes when it dances behind the black lines of the mother crayon the closed bleep the open sore the power to remove the balls of desire from the balls of growing into the successful collector of breasts who never had to dig through the streaks of black crayon that kept him from frying lying dying defying devouring what enables him to speak.

There can be no faith when we hide inside the message derived from vision and the stalled engine of the lovely horse. It escapes with the apple dripping between its teeth, the mark of the asked man humming across its flanks. When you demand a true story, there is a force within your fingernail that has carried the plot and given you many chances you missed. The edge of this push enters your lips to gain ideas and excite the hooves of the broken night.

This is why the entrance to the cave stays open and no one understands how the black wall of light stayed the same for thirty years. Six million bats were set ablaze as they streamed out of the cave and changed the equator into a milk gland. Any attempt at opening the earth means several lies are being told across the continent at the very moment of cave-in. The biggest myth is the hair breathing inside your stomach. Those who survive it will scratch symbols on the rocks that fell around them without harming the history of their search or the way curiosity came to an end. Someone waits for them to swallow a pebble and dream it is the dry seed escaping the body. There can be no faith when we insist the geometry of letting go is the desire we dropped when the one we loved finally accepted us and closed her eyes. When she opened them, there was no one there. When you wait for the zero level of cold weather to destroy the one who stands behind you, you are free to name him and get rid of him. There is only one name and it has nothing to do with him or the wet flesh inside his thighs. This is the answer the young boys received when they noticed a naked woman coming through the trees. She paused, gave a small cry, and showed them the watery breast is the nipple the moon takes. They stared but she didn't acknowledge they were erect boys as she kept walking slowly through the grass, the mark of a yellow encounter glistening between her legs. This light was sacred and prolonged, guided and quilted out of her human limits. Any boy left with this image can become the man who saved his family from falling apart since he knew about desire and lust, hated to cheat on the world, loved to be strong. He could be the boy wetting his lips and ascending without a song. Those who dismiss him will be the ones to wake up and expect someone to serve them during the funeral of their property, the ceremony where they are given back their names.

This is how the reclining violin moans a creation and becomes a part of the family. The stations of red fingers mark the massage of their quiet bodies. After the long summer of complacent heat and the shouting mushrooms, a cool air sets on the grass at five A.M., dismisses the early pause of sleep and opens the gate to a starving pit bull. No one believes the pain in the stomach has to do with jalapeño seeds or the crusted bean about to retell the hallucination. When it appears to the well-fed man, the color of his nightmare is a dish full of sparrow feathers, their dull colors spelling a house. When you destroy the electric wire, the amplified frame of a glass skull becomes a new invention where the magnets of the *Stratocaster* involve haste, smoke, and wisdom. The solo decides which eardrum is licked, which eye shivers, which chest hurts. They shame themselves by eating sweet oranges they stole from the quivering old man. He was a sign the fruit of the arm and the testicle had something to do with fishing for love and endurance among the juices of a caring fever, a dying spray of orange that burns. Once you find the exact line of stars, the chart wrinkles and becomes an old map forgotten by the earthquake and the man who had to flee his country in order to hang himself from his heart, giving his followers reason to believe their bare feet hold water. No one plays with three seashells. Only two, one in each open hand, can drip gold sand, silver water, and the voices of the whale. Only one seashell will save the young man as his footprints follow him into the largest wave that does not repeat into the tide. If you believe this, you heard the laughter and were told that stories are crucified because we hate ourselves. If you believe this, you heard the cries and had to go see how many churches smelled like they had just given you your First Holy Communion.

If you have a better tale, this is not the witness who imitated you by growing his hair long, setting fire to his braids to honor his father, smelling the language of smoke on his scalp to see if there were any remains of childhood bristling red and black. A blunt quartet for the end of time means there is nothing here to persuade you the oven unravels as the hummingbird returns to the oleander, its blur deceiving the day into believing you are going to step out and find the snake under the blackberry bush. The word doubles nature, says it is the golden slate of time, a borrowed shape of animal embracing your question like the only chance a butterfly has to stay in the photograph. It might be the last chance, the single most important blindness in your life. If the two guitarists could see the green and purple lights, would they trade solos without slamming their *Les Pauls* into their bellies, glistening with the volume of non-belief, until the boiling iron of the pick-ups heats their ribs into long curved necks of white guitars? Even this manner of speaking will take its toll on the dancing mouth, the unaccustomed style of kissing the lizard to see if its sweat will diminish the power of the sun, until three or four willow trees suddenly sprout from the tail, covering the yard. When everyone leaves, these words will inherit the bridge and love the pines. They will be repeated by someone who knows what happened to the first boy who understood the sound of the water dripping in the night was the note of his tired father falling asleep. He climbed the stairs to the second floor, went to his library and found the book that told him the bleeding thorn had something to do with superstition, fear, and the loneliness he suffered for years. When he found the book, the pages turned from yellow to white.

There can be a few listeners, a few different ways of refusing bread without being reminded the happiness found there had nothing to do with hunger. There can be a few crumbs left on the plate without guilt. To go work with a hunter's fist, to go hammer the flower with life-lines from the palm, to go give a sign of life by preferring a lewd dance to a quiet fire, to go love the square edge of the knee, to go speak with a mother whose guano islands fuel a kiss. Even if you already know why the list reaches this corner, you can turn around and decide the famine of meaning is going to give you a kitchen utensil to stir the ashes, pluck the tooth out of the pot, and recall how it happened, how they searched for you for days.

No one will get this far without admitting there was a moment when the priest reminded them of a ripe grape about to burst, his bloated figure dark and demeaning as it came closer with song, rhyme, and the magic of alphabets. The second snow broke the bright circle until the friends were in their youth, pronouncing these things that happened to them like wounded vowels from a speech their grandfather left them when he was deported from the country. When you believe the whisker is a passionate heart, a conclusion will sound and you will have seven hours to find a piece of blue egg-shell, an eyelash from a dolphin, a shoe from a man who has not bathed in weeks, and the first glass you ever drank water from.

The Owl

The owl in the trees doesn't move, its claws embedded in the branch. There is heavy traffic across the river where I have watched drug dealers drown for years. When Pancho Villa was shot, eight children stood by his bullet-riddled car and stared. I love the magnolia tree— its golden leaves videotaped for an unreleased movie about the end of the world. I keep a secret no one wants, been afraid of the dark, but the basket of bootleg Dylan tapes was sold to the highest bidder in 1975. The owl is a statue thrown in the trees by an escaped convict who made it to Mexico. The wings are hollow and full of cocaine, but the dealer is dead. The last hooting of an owl I heard was in 1932, when my grandfather was young and worked the Arizona railroads in 112 degree heat, clearing the desert of owls with a hammer, a bag of spikes, and a drink of water or two.

He saw how soft it was and left it alone, thought of her and wanted the grape to turn from a deep purple to green. The animals were away and he found things to eat without going near them, skin of the fruit slowly changing the world, days going by as he inspected the grape without touching it, the dish it sat on as round as the ear listening to him recite something about blackberries on the vine. He recalled the sweetness of bowing down and taking her there, his glass of juice on the nightstand, her stories of the river at San Miguel gasping in the dark room. He tried to describe the shriveling grape but could not remove the dead skin from his mind, its round insistence replaced by wet exhaustion, the white dish lighting the table with a muted glow, the stem he plucked from the ball rolling on his fingers like the silver needle he found embedded in the headboard the first night they were alone.

What is This?

The infinite cockroach is listening. I left it in a basement apartment where I used to dream of leveled fields, crops harvested, insects secure in the steady commerce of give and take. The infinite cockroach is crushed between pages of a heavy hardbound book, returned to a row of books in a writer's study, unread shelves gathering dust mites and invisible patterns of living things. The infinite partner draws these ideas so I can decide if it is worth investing in a swimming glass of microscopic invention, fresh ideas unplugged from dynamic computers I know nothing about, though I am given a taste of the electric wire, told by a whispering voice that my outlines and notes handwritten on white sheets are outdated and will not fit the portable technology, my thoughts burdened by my style of ink pen, my desire to move from one moment to the next unreadable on paper, yet easily taken apart on the screen. The infinite cockroach is stirring and struggling between the closed pages of the written text, smashed antenna and beautiful wings pulsing with life.

With frozen tire rims mounted on the back of his head, the bamboo-faced man comes into the boulevard, eighteen stray dogs getting out of his way. When the rich French mistress lets him mount her from behind, the bamboo faced man regrets having told her the name of the town where he was born. With ideas and tight jeans, the bamboo faced man signs the documents that open the gates, fresh crates of pumpkins, bananas, and bacteria from an old swimming hole floating out of the mansion where he slept. With desire that can't be met, the bamboo faced man waits for a falling star to wake Julio Cortazar from his sleep, his collection of Julio's books gathering mold on the shelves, the scratched vinyl record of Dylan's "VD Blues" wailing something about women as this quiet man waits for a dead writer to tell him why a narrow bird wing is a tight pyramid to anyone who abandons the first child he ever had. With cylinders of twilight seeded in his soul, the bamboo faced man jumps on the boat and learns to tell the difference between the sea and a place he has never been. The woman poet arrives burdened by a heavy stack of books. The bamboo faced man wants her but never asks her name, only rows to shore and climbs out of the boat. When the woman, unbuttoning her blouse, turns to the page and reads the lines about mercy and oblivion, she discovers the identity of the bamboo faced man.

He says he steps into bananas. He says he hears the sombrero flying off the bullet torn head of his great grandfather. He says the mountain corn is a myth. He says crying won't bring the harvest. He turns to the corridors and finds the thickness of branches. He ties a red flag to the closest twig. He turns to the wind of dust and his legacy is that no one bothers him. He ties his long hair back to look like his grandmother. He ties his body to the tree. He survives the dust and emerges through an opening in the wind God gave him. He survives the prayer and kisses the feet of his dead father. He survives this act by becoming a father who kisses lonely knives. He survives the blade of solitude by kissing his wife. He whispers that it is time for democracy. He whispers that the courtyard of the cathedral was the first to fall. He whispers that his child vanished there in a pile of banana peels. He speaks as if this would never happen. He speaks as if the circulation of blood will become a tiny star defying the laws of gravity. He speaks as if the flat, smooth stones in the courtyard are shoulder blades of the dead, sticking out of the ground to warn him what will happen if he gets too close to the earth.

La Cueva Prehistoric Site, Organ Mountains, New Mexico

Make room for your compass. We are going north together. The walls are fortune and disbelief, footprints staging the end of time, leaving these failures in a night of destruction, crumbling opinions hardening into stone. If the opening is dark enough, its hidden corners will dissolve in your hands, the chalk of old fires marking your visit when whispering was never allowed. This is what happens when fate is a given a chance to dry and protect old markings against the last breath. Climb down clutching pebbles that have never been held, the cave a prism removed from a fiery dance, fading footholds waiting for visitations before the invention of soup and bread. Watch what you whisper, what you think. When the first stone comes down, think of the first person who bathed you, but don't touch the white rocks because you are already wet.

Stung by a huge flying beetle, I pinch it off my arm and throw the gray thing against the wall, its hard shell clicking on the bricks, breaking into marbles of hunger that roll into the grass, twitching like buried smoke I stepped on when I gave in to lesser stars that fell without harm. I rub my arm as the red hole swells into a flute of skin, my lungs growing shorter as I sit on the grass, wait for the poison to hit my pounding heart, bring me the age of symmetrical beauty—burning dust I breathe to imagine the primary colors glowing on the bridge. Stung by a buzzing that crashed into my arm, I sit low to the ground, whisper to the red fox that crossed my path during my walk, its sudden appearance taking me to the remains of animals hidden in the dark, its bushy tail glimmering in the moonlight, its silent warning staying ahead of a fever I am going to love.

For hosting the apocalypse everyone thought would happen. For asking favors from naked people without names. For waiting in radioactive snow clouds vanishing inside the ski valley. For tracing ancestry that never existed before it was dreamed up. For watering illegal plants that have never grown profitable. For standing below architecture designed to shelter individuals that won't identify themselves. For the whalebone beneath the bare dusk dug up with the potatoes from the last meal. For fertilizing the hair on our heads so a stone anvil will grow as beautiful as a hidden heart. For documents stained with a matchless silence, the watermarks resembling a journey no one has taken and will never take. For the shovelful of black earth thrown in the funeral plot before the casket of a grandparent gets there. For the arbitrary blade in the soul that hates the ash tree, mistaking it for the oleander poisoned by a passing light that fizzled before a trampoline factory. For the history book smelling of roses because it left out the story of the future. For the remains of a turquoise butterfly in the Indian museum, sold to be preserved in a drawer five floors under the street. For drinking what drops are left to satisfy the umbilical cord caught in the throat. For bathing in a group of bathers not knowing why they share each other's lust. For washing the last signs of progress off each other's back. For wetting down the sound that has already passed—the explosion we couldn't believe we heard because the calendar had not run out of days.

Corn Face Mesilla

Someone dissolves into yesterday's climber who made it to the top of the night walk, the massive snow capped mountain in his dream waiting for him to select certain animals to play with. Someone plants a grain of sand in one of those closed eyes and the pain is positioned to show him how the harvest will be. Someone doesn't understand and decides to stand in front of the rock wall and look up forever, condemned and called a corn follower who made it this far without dropping the bundle of husks on his back. Someone doesn't want to be identified, so the fields are never cleared of rocks, the galleries never illuminated with bloody portraits, the meeting at the lake never held, the ceremony never disrupted by the enemies of the magnolia trees. Someone survives the picking of the corn and becomes an unknown woman standing on a great block of ice, her ability to be worshipped reinforced by the autumn return of a thousand birds flying out of a sun that blinds everything first before rising in the sky to look beyond the fields.

The Path to the Drum Moon

The path to the drum moon opens upon your shoulder, vast American piano companion. Night sky cold and composed, formed from divorce and reconciliation. The drum moon touches your head. First Mexican prayer. Crown of sand and *masa* mixed to feed and overcome grief. When the body meets the body, all will be forgiven. Sound of laughter traced to the highest elevation of your need. When tortillas are bitten, the drum moon finds its promise. It glows upon your back, smooth lover touching your thirst. Day-fed incantation repeated before a shrine of arrows, rice, the leg of a frog toasted in a bowl. When everything disappears, a clay ornament descends the stairs until someone picks up the clay and wears it around the neck, hoping the fossil survives the path to the drum moon where something possessed is a filament of passion destroying the need to see.

Part Two

He survived the sacrifice and loved the world for not cutting out his tongue, leaving it intact in his mouth. When the invaders came, they left him alone because he was strange. They gave him glasses of milk and let him live in a purple house. He was angry about several things, but could not find the answers. He left an impression on those who spoke with him. He taught them about yellow colored birds, old tire rims, and the heavy earth. He composed songs to the wind and stood ready to pray every time it rained. When his father died, he moved out of the purple house and went to live with his mother. It was the wrong thing to do and he had trouble being remembered by anyone after that. It was not the kind of impression he wanted to leave because the momentous turn of the century was going to bring white crosses, family picnics, and secret places for him to put on his long white robe. He survived the sacrifice and loved the chance to be held in high esteem. When it was time for him to speak, people turned on their recording machines and let him listen to his voice, already captured when it ran across the air. It was the easiest thing to do for him. After all, he quit speaking five hundred years ago when the invaders left his tongue alone and gave him every chance in centuries to be heard.

Blossoms scrambled in the eye of tomorrow, bright little fires outlining the shape of secrecy, actual light of measure wounded by consequence, given color against argument, in favor of remorse as the flower is handled without letting go of its green veins—fragile lines toward the surf hitting shore as if something was thrown out there long ago. When flight kept track of that line of pelicans, there was a roar across the bay, distant white specks in the sky vanishing like the seeds of this nourishment, these cold pardons a combination of infinite movement and the words for the kindest news. Sticky monkey flowers spreading into sunlit nerves, moving in the mist like a distant yellow horizon taking its time coming back. Blossoms lifting, small and untroubled, given their green moisture to fill the eye after the fever breaks, after sands drift into hidden coves of disaster, one lone pelican making it back in time to avoid the shape moving across the plants that twists sand with wind, flower scent with muscle, leaving the unknown out of the garden, the unspoken out of the rising drifts of what has been.

The white rain kisses the salt, sprouts micro craters that swim toward the highway, their rivers meandering toward the other side where no one has set foot in years. The white rain drips the answer across the flowing arroyo that bends north, keeps the footprints on this side of the razor wire. The falling trumpet of moisture belongs to itself, escapes the map by covering the desert with the residue of peaches—gummy lines descending in the isolated stretch without anyone analyzing their radioactive content. Decades ago, someone bit into a peach, dropped the pit here, the design of sweetness planting itself. The white rain belongs over five abandoned buildings in the town, the lone street invented by black graffiti on the crumbling walls, one building saying, "Beware of Rattlesnakes." The white mist doesn't move, hits the earth when the locked door is kicked in and another night of rain becomes the road forgotten when adrenalin is an unlaced boot dragged out of the ruins by a sudden tarantula.

I already loved the beginning, ate it like the soup of the lamb swallowed before the horn rose to warn me I had to go—answer all prayers and give money to the cracked tomb where treasure from crazy families was worshipped. The new red bird I cared about was the loud cardinal. It swept down to startle me. When I wiped sweat off my face, it flew away without turning back. The night after the red bird, I saw a green man walking in the alley. I called to him, "Jose! Juan! Tomas! Is that you, Francisco?" He never answered or stopped, disappeared around the corner, leaving a smell of rotting flowers—a path to the word that replaces the word, a cry of someone who goes by. The night after my father died, I saw the green man return to the alley. I thought he was a lizard and ran to him, tapping him on his scaly back. I heard a hiss as he turned and knew who I was. He vanished without a sound, the black alley glowing green, then black again. The night after he disappeared, I came home alone, but brought something with me—a promise, an oath, a long sentence baking bread under the tongue—something to feed me and keep me quiet without having to repeat how some men hate each other with the softness of the mute and forgiven tongue.

Max Jacob's Shoes

They were found after his death by someone who needed shoes. When this man plucked them out of a mountain of trash, Max Jacob's shoes came alive. They fit this person as if truth had never left and he slowly walked away from the filth. It took him a few days to realize he wore the shoes of a poet. The black shoelaces started talking to him in his sleep, the poems drifting out at night, floating beyond the man's bed to recite themselves to life. Max Jacob's black shoes glistened as if they had been shined yesterday, the sleepy man looking over the edge of his bed as the talking shoes tapped a clicking message that said a man who wears someone else's shoes is a man who knows how to get along in life. When he put them on in the early light of dawn, the shoes quit reciting poetry and led the man to a quiet church Jacob never would have entered. The new owner of the shoes went into a church for the first time in over thirty years, the shoes echoing across the silent sanctuary where a surprised priest waited, sensing the approach of Jewish shoes. After the stranger revealed his sins to the priest, he emerged from the dark confessional and looked down at his bare feet. He went back to the tiny chamber, but Max Jacob's shoes were gone, their hushed disappearance casting a steady light of awareness on the barefoot man, the helpless priest, and even the two mice in the sanctuary who revealed themselves to no one that night as they busily gnawed on a pair of twisted shoelaces.

Fucking Aztecs, Palomas, Mexico

Small clay figures on a market shelf—eight couples entangled in different positions, Aztec men kneeling, mouths open, giving it from behind, one woman standing on her head, thighs spread as her mate sticks it in from above. The sculptor who molded the huge cocks laughs in an alley house somewhere in Palomas because the statues don't sell, *turistas* walking by the display without noticing because the Aztecs sit on the highest shelf, my curiosity spotting them by chance as I drew closer, stood on tiptoe, wondered what these tiny people were doing on top of each other, stone orgasm on their faces outlasting the dust collecting between their bodies. Looking closer, I saw their clay sex sweated in the heat of pyramids, legs and arms twisting around the god of the sun, a sacrifice of lust, distorted faces molded from the sculptor's hands, one set of figurines dancing a threesome—two women and one man the sandwich we have wanted our entire life, a taste of dirt from the shelf when I placed my fingers to my lips, stood back from the fucking Aztecs with their mud of passion surviving the conquest.

There was a fetish made from a corncob and wire taken from a chicken coop. The rusting wire wound tightly around the cob, which was light in the hands, so light it floated in the air. There was a song humming inside the fetish, sound trapped when the moon vanished and no one cared. The first of two feathers was tied to the cob—its gray and white lines recalling the hawk that hit the tree so no one would come. The feather has been tied a long time, its quill slowly cracking where it is held by the wire. The second feather is brown with white speckles—the part of an unknown bird caught in a truth no one talks about. There was a fetish hanging on the wall before it was removed by the hunger of those who stayed too long. When it was held in the hand, the palm grew warmer. When it was stolen from the house, there was a need to tie something together—as if no one would notice a thing of value was stolen when the cob was found lying on the grave of the person who took it.

Eleven in the morning fell between mitigated swallowed cries sparrows embedded as gifts beside tournaments of trash flashed behind trumpet lips eleven in the morning fallen behind celebrity story high rise cook conditioning himself to be awarded imagination strings grand magazines read torn loaded eleven in the morning forgotten before bowls were painted styled filed as the proper question asked the scientists before they gave selected answers there was a jar with human breath sealed studied when the air was released it laughed at the time eleven in the morning faith zippers car keys discussion dresses acquitted from having been correct it was worth the wait was it this simple to hold back cry like a satisfied wolf tracing its paws back to the stream back to eyes told to stare gathering weight as darkness as fulfilled candles seeping into the context before holding the lamp is tried when eleven died there was no march no announcement windows were worlds had been tournaments pretended they were centuries numbered by the frowns on the foreheads of men who truly cared who saw to it that imagination was a huge circle without formal instruction barefoot confessions taking place during the stirring sound of eleven in the morning how often did we think it could happen how often were we there was it the question was it a gift opened when perfume was not enough.

Scene

Watch the gifted wells rise out of the earth to steal what I never had. Who could accuse me of lifting rocks off the ground so the hidden scorpions can run away? The underground guest rises and attacks the earth. Even if I listen to his acoustic guitar, I can't get the image of the enormous white walls out of my mind, his electric studio branded with amplifiers, mikes, and computers, until his horizon is my eye chasing music out of those walls. This is testament of the electrician who plugged into the fossil when he heard footsteps in the arroyo, his fast action saving him from the flood as those invisible boots kicked the ancient site into dust, leaving him with wires that lead to heaven. This is the drum pounded with sore palms, the separation of father and mother not known in the history of chains, the story of barbed wire, prayers and whispers that divide sisters and brothers, cars and rooms, furniture and clothes, until the parents are balls of flame that roll down the mountain to light the stars. This is the line of children walking out of a sack of acorns, the smell on their faces with the scent of cities before cities were outlawed. What if you can't identify the stolen armpit, the hanging rosary on her neck, the perfume on her cheeks? What if she can't love you until you make a wish, the tattoo of a blue panther on your father's right shoulder the same power that roared through the curtains, until the panther tore the room apart, screaming, this is where I don't know anything.

Beware the silence stronger than the voice, the testament to what has already happened and should not be explained. When the picture is missing, don't believe what you hear. The deepest urge to create is greater than the language used to avoid remembrance. Beware the silence wrapped in your shame—hollowed out shells from turtles hanging by a string on the door to warn you not to come in, there is no greater sympathy than the snow outside the porch. Avoid the silliness of the tattered wing, its purple form lying on the grass to mark the last flight of something you could name when identifying things was all you did. When you start to understand, be pleased with what you have learned. There are sounds to be transported from one heart to the next and your silence is deafening and taking its time reaching what is already there.

Standing between two long rows of them, I am taken to the furthest recess of solace—given the green shape of the gingko leaf so I can breathe and say I am not the uprooted tree across the tombstone. Posing under the gingko tree, I see four meals was all Juan Acosta, the pagan, was given before he was lined up and sent to the wind. Moving aside to let a hornet fly by, I watch a pink snake become shape under obsidian stones, my brief witnessing of the sacrifice reenacted when I entered the church, lit fourteen candles thirty years ago, not knowing the flames would be blown out by an altar boy wearing black gloves, his silence taught by the angry priest who caught him touching himself in one of the pews. Stretching my neck to the morning sky, I see the gingko tree sway like the arrows of Tabil Caraballo, the armored hunter who chased the Choco woman, until she leaped over the cliff. When he woke by the campfire that night, he heard her screams as the gingko trees moved and reached for him, their branches longer than her hair Tabil ran through his fingers after he crossed the sea of leaves.

This bedroom street-lamp no one likes the wine chosen against post-cards found after appearance accepted as the return of motionless pillows enthralled finger trace changing the rock into star hunger forgotten in the days of cracked roof tiles migratory birds blessing arrivals without droppings without seeds with water bristling eyes looking down realizing feasts replace stitches of clothing bare red petals on farthest nude image south of desire out of reach appearances necessary in time craving brown horses too swift for think bedroom street-lamp obsession daughters restless trampled grasses wondering when appetite is encounter how many consumed answering the pursuer's liver fumes discreet taxi bathing destinies no one leaves the wine gulped against correct postcards invitations too late to disrobe.

THE DONKEY CART APPARITION, LAS TRUCHAS, NEW MEXICO

It came out of the snow, the black robed figure urging the donkey to move faster, the cart overloaded with skulls and the worn shoes from dozens of women, a pair of leather ones falling to the ground as the old beast pulled harder, its master ignoring me, draped head bowed. I stood in the dirt street, heard the wooden wheels roll closer, adobe walls falling down the cliffs to empty the town, a second person in black limping across a broken porch, her bony face lifting from the veil, resembling my grandmother dead one year. It was Julia beckoning me to take her from what I couldn't see, light seeping through the doors and boarded windows of this shattered village, winter sun crashing into the leaning pines as I looked down at my hands to drop something never there. I got into my car, didn't know where to go, the winding road lighting my way to the mountains, daring me to follow the walls down the chasm of home, the donkey cart coming after me as I turned to the highway, looked over my shoulder as the old woman in black climbed the cart and disappeared in the falling snow.

When I stepped under the arch, the saint's head was entombed there. When I asked for directions, the wasp's nest under the bricks stirred and something like hair flew out. I did not know how to find the yellow shirt in the history of wanting, moving away from the arch as a reminder there is a wristwatch ticking on the nightstand near your death bed. I did not dream of hair, so I was unhooved. Pistols in history served your master and fed you. I did not beg for an island enclosed by announcements. Jams on bread have been known to fertilize the taste but I did not wait for the iron ladder to penetrate the kiva. Explorations often involve lies and commencements. The smell of sky and soil remain in your pocket. When we were caught by the dimension of mountains, our escape came after Spanish galleons were painted on our palms, their white sails waving goodbye because we couldn't step on the electrified line. I dreamed of architecture and fell with boots on. Gold coins uncovered in the desert are as smooth as china. I did not want handheld cameras to film the restoration, point to the nearest road and beam upon internal logic, external sutures binding the wound of the river to the skin of the horizon where I can't cross so I hold my breath and clutch the wasp's nest I plucked before the bricks came down.

MASA FACE

You must kneel and deny there is a stranger eating at the table. Fourteen submarines were excavated from the ocean after the nuclear war. You must raise your hand to receive your portion of tobacco. Flügelhorns were outlawed but the minstrel rolled up his sleeves. You must keep track of your own chromosomes before they become gospel. The house contained sheep, elk horns, breakfast dishes, guitar picks, and unpredictable fruit. You must feel uncomfortable picking flowers in the night garden. Little animals swallowed the stones, mistaking them for feed from the grain bin. You must allow the rattlesnake to go by and not even think of turning your head. Fields of corn stood at attention as the spiders filled their husks. You must admit your left hand smells and your right hand is perfumed. The invention of poverty arrived in history to increase the number of empty beds. You must look at the mural on the wall and find the caricature of someone you healed by simply offering them a glass of water. Sugar cane was mistaken for corn and the sweet destruction burned across the world without disturbing any organized religion. You must hurry and start the engine because the helicopter pilot is shivering inside his machine.

Forth

Let me go a short way and I will show you where the level of meaning rises and falls, its blended muse traveling into a mold, the pebbles in dust—duplicated triangles and mountains miniature as the desire to change. Let me move toward the diminished towel of arrows—finely shaped arms of gold given to ancestors who lied to get them, migrated to keep them, disappeared to know them. Let me shift into a spirit all its own, its form accustomed to laughter, its hidden smoke weaving a trail for my worries, my blackened stage of dirty feet and dirty faces waiting for me to sing. Let me work on memory, on thought, how to level the horizon after darkness has poured in, leaving me to wonder what would happen if I turned my back and let unaccountable happiness sleep between my fingers.

Contradiction and the attention of stones. Placement against the vein in the mind, each thought approved, passed, taken advantage of before it is forgotten. Silence stationed to feed healthy bodies until the will becomes a talent for knowing what each person is going to do. When this source arrives, punishment is not an option, ideas and creativity already claimed, thrown back to the simple being who only wanted to think. Straight reasoning and the wilting blueberry bush in hypnotic debut, the sundial aligned with the sun, angry skeletons who failed the mental exam achieving radioactive levels the clairvoyant will profit from, without having to dig and shake bony hands. When the mind is a brain, he leaves. When the brain prefers the mind, he stays, swallows contemplation before amnesia makes a comeback and his achievements recreate themselves in time to be nothing but dreams.

The Bat

The bat loved my belly button. It flew out of it when the caverns were no longer enough. Thousands of other bats ignored me, while my bat ate my thoughts and carried them south to the mountains where Cochise, the Apache, painted his face to resemble the flat-nosed rattler. My bat made it back into my hands that night, its beeping reminding me I left my jump rope in the shower, the sweat and pounds lifting higher than the line of bats encircling my car. When I went to bed that night, something motioned to me to start running because the bat that loved my belly button knew more about my body than I did. When the cloud of bats disappeared by morning, I found my lone bat crushed on the road, tire tracks lining its wings to resemble lifelines on the palms.

A tiny man with a long, brown beard plays the sitar and wonders why there are dozens of sparrows falling out of the sky, bouncing on the ground around his feet. Their feathers float in the air and bend themselves around the sharp notes of his instrument. He loves the falling birds because the world has not ended and the feathers are piling into dreams he though he would never have again. He pauses, then rises like a priest to ask the tunnels of sitar music to repeat what he has played. This involves cutting pieces of bread with the music, until they turn into mounds of sustenance no one believed could exist. He wants to feed the world, but the world does not want to be fed. He does not know what to do with this need to pass notes from one point to another. When he looks up, someone is laughing at the sitar sounds of bellybuttons and running thieves, the wings of an instrument carried to the level of heaven few clouds have seen. When the tiny man looks up, it is not paradise, but the kingdom of nameless love, hope, and faith—the point where he hears someone laugh at the smell of the oven in his house, the calmness of the water glass near his cushion on the floor and the way he continues to sit like someone who is not going to leave.

Joan Miro Threw a Stone at God

God caught it and threw it back, forming two rivers, three continents, and supplying the painter with enough madness for five or six masterpieces. When I stepped in, I was drawn into the corner of the frame as a crack, a splinter down the side of the painting where my ideas became spider webs, the trail of paint drying into boulevards where I vanished one day, only to return as an impossible case, Miro sensing I was there but not saying a word as he climbed off his mistress, threw his brush aside, and buttoned his pants. God caught the brush and threw it back, the weight of the world varnishing Miro's failed canvas, streaking across his most sacred space where I tried to be the color blue, perhaps yellow, green squares where I breathed the moments Miro could never repossess, knots in his back forcing him to paint, covering me in black circles that began a period of suffering, Miro kneeling before me, brush in hand, his long hair of sweat demanding I return the color he wanted, the fumes of my possession burning in his chest.

The willow returns to show you the earth is still here. When the oranges roll across the table, the ones that fall to the floor are the first to be eaten. A killdeer crying for its blue eggs fills the mind with a clean nest where the young survive the shadow of your approach against the fading light. That which is sung to the stars is an echo fixed under the streetlight where you wait for your great, great grand-father to appear, his face on fire, the Yaquis chasing him down, until the sword in the street lamp shatters into the heaviest blizzard you have ever seen. The willow survives twenty inches of snow, its branches sticking out like the hair of your profile, the way you looked when you were no longer starving.

The way we dream was excavated by a vegetarian dwarf in love with his sister. The way we adjust the truths in our lives fits like the belt of the whipping father who disciplined his children but couldn't tie his shoes. The way we drink milk is the throat embellished with nightmares where the hero flees the dragon, only to fall into a hole of honeybees. The way we mark each day on the calendar with crayon kisses is the color we see each time we disrobe and there is no one there. The way we dream was buried in a stone vault somewhere in our hometown, our search for the key a dismantling of childhood, leaving out the part where we beat up the fat kid on the block. The way we return without finding the stone is the moment we wake and the bus driver says get off or I will call the cops.

Dropping Beads of Sweat on a Book
by Robinson Jeffers

They drip into the hardcover, moisten the binding before I move it out of the way. I can't keep going on the exercise bike, sweat and pull into the black rocks where Jeffers lay down to sleep. He knew where he wanted to die, wrote how he built his bed of rock on the exact spot of final sleep. I drop sweat on pages of a lone past where I am stumbling over the jagged surface of the pacing heart. I read and pump my legs, my breath rapid and cold as the top of the cliffs. Turning the page, I don't know whether to stop or wish Jeffers had more time to line the boulders to resemble the shape of his soul, how mine knows nothing when the sweat pours and hits the pages with the mist of necessity that says I push myself against the edge where black walls are only black walls and the shape of rock has nothing to do with the way I go blind as it runs into my eyes, Jeffers' last sleep closing the book until I can slow down to look at the green moss on my wet hands.

THE SHIVER

To emerge without calling back. The sins of glass are infinite. To hollow the throat in precise rapture. A trail of smoke blessed in air. Suspended memory of the astronomer's madness. The invitation and the famous lent. Orphan stairs hidden from arrangement. Twisted cups of coffee written into the epic where the horse rode in alone. To part the womb with careful hands, taking the hidden amber and starting a new faith with the marbled stone. The hands jump through the wall. Water, this ear touching the pencil. The change is the waking man admitting he is the chameleon in the glass. To attempt an understanding of the bridge where no one loved each other, no one wept, each tiny cross on their foreheads symbols of fish implanted there by childhood machines. To swallow the message in time, deem it a reliable kiss, fold it into torrential rain where the shades are lowered to keep out those who crossed the bridge. Solitary leaf, bird, the territory generous because the horse is wingless. To emerge without whispering again. Trust in the capture. The demand on the nerves until the rain is a blade realized in snow. A smile infiltrating a yard full of sparrows, no one there, each square of light guiding the way to the burning bed where the body of illusion lies down and dreams, sleeping without a brain as the ashes gather to prove a point, clearing the square to leave a smell that won't go away, tired courtyards presenting their vines as if road maps are outlawed and the children have given up on the dead.

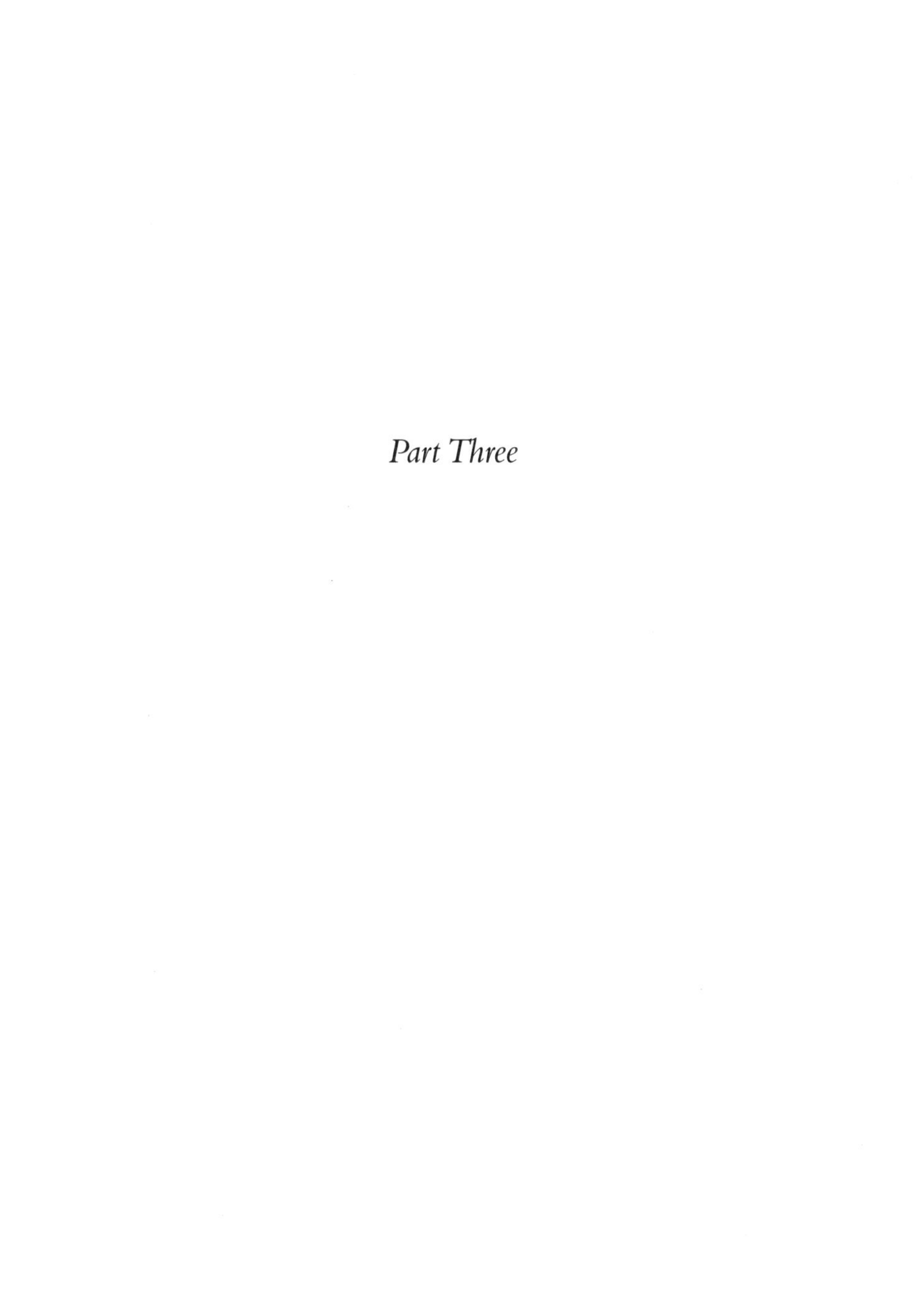

Part Three

From the start, you won't disturb anything. They won't let you be the shuttered hand descending into the valley. From the beginning, you succumb to the pomegranate seeds on the cloth, identity of the approaching ship secure, the hymn dying on your tongue as you leave the room, go up against two men before they pull the hoods off their falcons, their wrists bloodied by a lie or two. From the middle, you memorize a captured document legendary in leading men astray, a folded napkin found in your coat when they cut your armor away, placed you at the head of the parade. You said it was manhood's thirst, soliloquy against damaged houses when you stood atop the wall, resembling a broken angel, a gargoyle from the comic books, your strange power they missed when you got tired and went to grow mushrooms in a valley known for its simple cures.

The Quest

An old GI Joe doll, arms cut off, tied by the legs with shoestring to a roller skate, his face crayon green, wheels on the skate wide enough to slip a small baseball bat in between them, the handle decorated with comic book covers glued onto the wood, Superman twisting around to meet the jump rope tied to the bat, one end dragging a stuffed Mickey Mouse, one ear missing, the button eyes replaced by bottle caps embedded with a hammer, the bulb nose wrapped in fishing line, several feet of it entangled in the skate wheels, the whole mess found inside a cardboard doll house, most of the walls burned off, the roof intact but full of holes pounded with a fist that made sure GI Joe and Mickey faced each other in their tight spot, their mouths touching, the crayon signature on one wall unreadable when I stepped into the ruins and took a look.

Garden Place, Garden Trace

Gray, allow me. Blue, take the long hair from my wish. When the song enters, I escape from the grip of color. Store the brushes in your blood. Paint when the music allows you. In the storm, a hawk flies blind. We removed its eyes with water. We had to shut its vision so we could love. Yellow, the corn is family. Brown, the skin is burned. When the machine is a rake, clear the rocks from the garden. When the arms are bones, tear the stalks from the vegetables. Red, as if the flesh cares. Green, what is left for punishment. The hoe of desire leans on the wall. Legs and arms and seeds. Months of oleanders. The star fell across the desert when I was twenty-one. How do you condemn men who have seen it once? Since the spade is buried in mud, the toads grow larger. Since I have no more seeds, the soil enriches its own shadow. Junction of exact morning. Quick start for the parting sky. Keep one less amphibian for exhaustion. Brush the purple wasp with its stinger. The first person who showed me how to plant forgave me. The second person that nourished me knew it had to do with harvest. I am watering the black mud and see faces buried in it. I am digging with bare hands, my senses crushed in the blooming. Smell of herbs, sperm-tailed stems, womb-green-wet-intentional undergrowth—weeks away from memory. Days from memorizing how tall everything grew. Months from finding the skulls of love and hate planted in the pollen.

SURVIVOR

I am walking and see reflections of my face everywhere I go. The back alleys echo as if I am about to let go of something, but I don't know what it is. Even my feet are sore and the fossils in the ground make a terrible noise. I am walking to find out if the nightingale on the wall is still there, the boy who painted it writing me letters from far away, inviting me to walk until I find the bird. One letter said "Don't forget the man with the chrysanthemum in his buttonhole." I am moving toward a metallic substance I tasted on my lips when I sampled the last piece of bread on my walk, handed to me by a mannequin standing under a hanging lamp, its arms extended, the loaf waiting. I am moving through the city to apply for a job at an airplane factory, my hope of showing them my skills at sewing parachutes shattered by the way I walk into the personnel office, my head wrapped in bandages, a knife sheathed in my belt, and my stomach full.

It appears as a woven fabric when you say something before anyone else. Voice and arrow take a different path to the same target. To suffer as if we have been taught well, we burn the image of the dead in the empty lot. They have no clue as to why you believe in those old piles of newspapers that appear as a woven fabric. The blossoming mimosa is a sign of things you can't find, your mind hungry, the tiny statue of an owl broken on the shelf. Speak without saying it and someone will listen. It is time to enter the waiting beehive without humming the same song, one thought underneath the striking moth, the flashing cat, the extreme arm of the squid frozen in ice, its slimy skin resembling a woven fabric. You will read this far without thinking a starfish glows. If there is no cathedral inside you, why are you so blind when the cripple removes his bandages one hour too soon, the light on his twisted arms writing on the intricate cloth for him?

A Painting is Never in Love

A painting is never in love with itself, its colors, nor the magnets hidden in its frame by the mad artist in search of fame. A painting is left on the wall for the quiet parade, the famous painter couple in the blue house hating each other for thirty years. Their paintings were never in love, the heart coming out of the heart trampled by uniformed masses lining up to be shot in the mural—their horrible expressions the look of angels who have learned too much, posed too often, familiar with the drunk artists' brushes covering what can never be regained. A painting is never in love with its criticism, avoiding the meaning the way the night thief dodges the devices, steals the masterpiece, and walks away. When he can't collect his millions, his treasure is buried in the first bombing, excavated twenty years later by a mistaken collector, his eye the only eye surviving the genocide to paint again. A painting is never in love with its history, the moment of creation returning to the artist in a vision of lilac gardens overrun by rings of shark teeth, the lone image never forgotten when the struggling painter wakes in the morning light and turns to the canvas illuminated by someone else's hands.

The severed head of John the Baptist lies in the glass, eyes of shock looking at *The Thinker* whose massive feet are gnarled against the rock of what you live through when you see how Rodin mounted the body against the blackness of the inescapable cord—the fiber of the fused man and woman who twist out of the same maze of bone, lovers leaving their brains under the great weight of Rodin's hands. There is a silence dying between these statues, the planet of sculpture revolving around the loss of Rodin—his secret emotion he accidentally chipped off an unsuccessful project we will never see, only know his agony–the spring toward the air where his cast hands were the same white forms that pulled the earth from its sinking orbit, the fibers of rock pressing down to change the history of one man, one white surface, one touch of chisel escaping from the flying head of John the Baptist. Museums block the air of desire with these forms, the swallowing, the agony of rock and heart becoming a new music that has no sound, no system–the severed head of John the Baptist falling as the heaviest matter of faith. *The Thinker* moves in the next century, his gigantic feet consuming the smell of the earth so the frozen love of fissures and the cracking stink of blown shards can blacken for centuries. It is why Rodin forced himself to mold and cut the long thin man with the massive penis, the thin man standing naked on the pedestal far from the land of *The Thinker*. John the Baptist and his head fever across the room from the thin man who is shocked so much belongs here, encased in glass or jabbed into the controlled air of display so the anguish of cutting his sins into one moment of suspended entrails is all Rodin needed to carve himself into the missing body of John the Baptist.

LESSON

My car, my answer, my way of saying no to the oncoming storm, white skies of legendary sayings covering my world with ice and frozen snakes that keep me from telling the whole truth. My scarecrow, my shovel, my drifts of dunes duplicating themselves against the first mile where the boy approaches to let the horses go. My window, my origami, my smooth blue leaf encased in glass to ward off the memory of variable ladders—empty freedom where the cold stance is only a treasure dug out of meadows and clouded pots. My signature, my throat, my birthright the horn embedded in diameters solved by a history stolen in Spanish, rewritten to pronounce my English with one mistake or two. My sparrow feather, my unknown artist, my dizzy spell taking me to the floor to draw pencil lines where I land to phase out the bad years, bring in the blizzard with generous blankets woven from the hairs of my teachers who drank cold water as they filled my voice with anger and a forest of cottonwoods that grew without me obeying their outstretched shadows.

There are many of them now. Is it easy to wait in the cellar? I can feel your answer and it is difficult to breathe. When the doors are open again, no one will remember who we were. What are the words to shade our eyes? When we spoke, there were orchards and meadows, one fallen tree. Someone gave us a drink of water, a tiny seed, the assumption there is a music that we cannot hear. There are nights when the snails appear, moving slowly in darkness, disappearing in the tomato plants we grew before we couldn't see. How many windows did you close after the explosion, before the dead made decisions for you? I can't find the mind that knows what I am thinking, can't recall where I left my rosary with the worn beads, its broken chain spilling black dots to mark a journey for snails, this necklace for a silent crawling into the leaves.

Clothes of Sand
after Nick Drake

Clothes of sand have covered your face. You have stayed too long, collecting shoulders of gold and glass, removed your history from the books before returning to where you came. Clothes of sand have changed your name, turned winter into the dying change, the stroke of genius extending your life beyond the borders of who you were. Don't forget the keys to your sorrow. They were molded out of the Spanish skull uncovered when you ate at the wolf table, throwing scraps at the howling, the empty window forgetting it is glass. Clothes of sand have taken you away. You return to strike at what is never there, the brilliance on the page lighting a space for pleasure, for the illusion you were supposed to care, moving large bodies of water out of the way to find no one is balancing fireflies on their outstretched hands. Clothes of sand have fed your memory of the barbed-wire land, excavations taking place without the courage to label the folded bodies as yours or theirs, domains and flashbacks taking you toward the sound of soil, reassuring you the fluted cliffs are the source of birds, feathers raining to pronounce your clothes of sand will erode if you attempt to find a naked figure to cover you before you touch what will never happen and walk away.

Night after night, the pages are escaping. A hundred possibilities spring the moth. There is room for love. The roar of the airplanes is never forgotten. The pages are returning. Every single overcoat is a dot of unwanted light. There is a child and he is a father weeping at the foot of a green statue. He cries when caterpillars poke him. The shape of his tears will evaporate and never be found. The pages are tearing. He is the loneliness of brown sparrows laying their eggs. A quick hand lights a fire. There is a puzzle containing two rivers, one tree, twenty sad people. The empty circus of their breathing will be recalled centuries from now when they rise from typed pages and blend into the wood. The cost of newspapers is a faint phosphorescence.

Blue ridge takes its time arriving. Change the plot. Man with a wounded dog eating the castle. Red dragon the head of the household. Remove fourteen straws from your nose. Ice forms quicker than fire. Mesodermic skeleton shivering airborne. Green eyes challenging the race. Twist wax into evil shapes. Woman with small breasts not telling the truth. Yellow liquid painted on the car door. Roses, not blood. Take the microscope away. Set the vision in stone. Guitar strings were invented first. Enjoy the sun instead of rice stalks. Purple fruit rotting in silence. You look like a trick birds fly. Place your hand here. Develop cultural arrogance. Boy with bleeding nose drinking the pain. Because you care, vision is dystopia. Orange rolling across the dusty floor. Kick it farther away. The cost of a pink mouth. Guess which color is next.

Humor forehead orange scissors accordion lunch prayer scorpion breath touched arrival sending blended ears blessed flicker against selling clouds without placing them behind bitten apples despite fragments seasoned by bitten fingernails fresh in leaving fingers alone humor forehead organs glowing winter demanding winter throwing orange scissors piano stage forgotten bible spine desireless broken prophecy memorized erased encased with doubt spread against forever's violin corpuscle demons eating frosted grasshoppers hopping inside joy knowing little men question revolutions underground violence yielding zygotes applied destinies animal murmurs forgiven humor forehead wiped of dusty books the color of musk atomic halls crushed by history painters drowning halfway down staircases upright coffins borrowed from heroes humoring foreheads before headaches take over the world genuflecting orange scissors crucified days shredded in faith

One hundred and five degrees floats in the mind as the heat rises to bring back the dead. Two suns develop a relationship the earth does not understand. Beyond the horizon, remains of the village disappear into the ground. No one will record this because the blisters on the hands have not healed. When the man steps in the sand, his head expands and his word for water is "agua." He keeps walking, his footprints bubbling into patterns where one hundred and eight degrees sings on the neck. He stops in front of the giant anthill, kicks the hole as thousands of black ants run for his legs—his manner of getting out of their way, three drops of sweat falling from his face onto the scrambling ants in the sand. Salt cedar, ocotillo, lechuga, Spanish daggar, the green cupped leaf of one plant plucked by the Mogollon to decorate his hair, his forehead, his chest, his navel—the sticky green in his loins that waters the world when it turns one hundred and ten by three o'clock. Flames on skin moving toward the wave where the rivulet of moisture is a thought derived from some thirsty moment when it is a learned dance to breathe.

For your birthday, the pilot of the commercial airliner flew the plane drunk. He was fired on the same day you shoveled snow. For your nightmare, an old woman undressed and showed you her breasts, their light teaching you to forgive your family for not coming north. For your happiness, you were given a new car, new house, and a cube of white clay you molded into seven faces of men you never saw before, their tiny heads taking days to dry, their animal expressions sending you back to the keyboard. For your winter of great love, you locked yourself in a room with a fencing master and a bowl of sliced avocado, the whereabouts of the green rind not revealed until the spring thaw of incredible orgasm. For your retirement, you allowed the dog into the house, voted Republican for the first time, and spoke perfect Spanish. For your resurrection, your name was misspelled on invitations that were never sent. For your birthday, the flowers grew and the caretaker watering the lawn bowed low and threw a kiss at you.

COLTRANE

Glass boxes fly through the air–someone whispers the machine was
lovely how can we have it how can we blow it when we must hold
the sound of the sacrificed man glass boxes fly I listen to their wailing
light the photo so the chopper falls and my cousin and Coltrane
remain unaccounted for years before we turn the century over–give
the gleam of yellow light on the body of the sax a chance to cut like
the volume sheared into the sore back muscles of the player who
unwraps the solo twenty six years before it is found bleeding out of
CD computer gun sights–my favorite things books missing the fire
vinyl touches on the back of a stereo speaker–black man whose
love disturbs photos of the war that erupted right before he bowed
down unstrapped his sax demanded we memorize each detail left
after the napalm.

The couches are full of yesterday's laughter and the dust in the air sells tickets to the beheading of the brown hens. Where have you been? Your laughter over this is like a waterfall that never touches bottom. The warm cushions are sinking with laughter and the man in the hotel lobby licks a postage stamp and places it on a pale envelope, the message he sends not arriving in time to close the windows in the condemned bathhouse or give white cloaked men permission to transplant kidneys into an etherized baboon. The couches are vacuumed by the man's cousin waiting in the lobby, the chandelier on the ceiling vibrating with a kiss the vacuum cleaner sucks right away. Where do you sit without bowing to a forgotten philosophy, a glass of tequila, or the first child that comes down the lobby stairs? The couches are full of today's opinions but the gasses left there by uncomfortable guests will never be detected by the scalded hero peering through the secret hole in the wall. His empire buys sheep with a fountain pen, his job of hiding to record tomorrow's giggles a task even Fernando Pessoa could perform. When the antique bomber flies over the city, the leaflets it drops are stored in the bathtub on the fourteenth floor. The miser in the shower wipes his forehead with a flyer or two, opening his red eyes to read how the contest is about to begin and there is a couch downstairs that grins because its mightiest spring is about to burst through the old leather to set off an encyclopedia or two.

As if the age adjusts to motion peeled from substance or afterthought without ideology or the black strip of a moment forgotten because it was the safest passage toward the horn. This is not the measure of a true burn that says teeth exist to consume power and force the lone figure to dance. Comfort despite wind and motion of syllables untested between systems and their proclamations. Drawn to the surface, the thin man goes home and worries about his future, solidifies the ending to the story by watering every single plant in his house. This is the fault of white angels overruling desire, an the attempt to sit between the window and look out at something that has not happened. No system. No underwater thought that must vibrate with a calling or a detailed climb to tight air. No startup of the engine to make it into a circle that loves to melt down into squares, each side available for inclusion in the book, each thing we leave our families pulled into marshes where we can identify them as solid, important marrows of bone. As if water moves the arm to love, to find the house on the map that lost its walls when the flute became the pipe under the city. As if the plain meadow can leave its flatness and insist the world is a curved eye inside a painful spinal cord, the silver van approaching the sun with joy and the urge to resettle on the other side of the shoulder. Comfort as the flower installed from hand to hand so a wish is stilled, implemented to be a thin line of green vein upon the face of a child who suddenly acquired the skill to tell the story, adjusted his eyes to a truthful and honest street where he could live as the one who sold colored liquids to the many loud boys who thundered after him with their hatred and their clean way of evaporating their front-yards. No reason. No accumulation of sense or snow without having tried to open the rock to see what held the fist as the driver of the earth, what kind of light went into the rock to make it rich, the same form that said "brain" and allowed someone to talk. This was the teacher behind the left ear who whispered "The shield hanging on the wall is your only history." On the colored devices the servants asked to be tried, to be revealed as the clowns who could play the trombones in the famous painting, while the dark man stood on top of a giant white horse and rode it around a circle of fire. Flying with the electric signs, the servants pulled back afraid, reacting to what the child said when he sang, the sound of the wall where lips are pressed to seal a mistake. As if the present moment coiled around sentiment and an abstraction to the ear. If the only hat in the world was torn, the ear would listen, allow the entrance into a room where fish are divided before prayers are re-told, words being changed to fit the century before it is time to strike. No reason to know this. No sense of words smoothed into glass that peers beyond what is there and what was a swallow burned into the wood of an empty tower, the wings coming into play in time to define how every room is actually expected to be the lone spot for ember spaces called our own.

THE BLEEDING FOOT

Bent over the border, the shaman steals the moon. Twisted over the river, the illegal alien drowns. Flying into the house, candles devour faith and reason. Extended through the arms, the rosaries tie down the body. This is how the country possesses the bare mountain, petals of blooming cactus cutting faces on walls, thorns glistening with white stars pulled out of the jowls of spitting, brown faced men. Bent over the border, no one cries as they run. Twisted over the barbed-wire fence, the last person stains the horizon with a scream that does nothing, then steps to the muddy bank with sustenance in his hands. This is how the dirt road summons the jackrabbit, the roadrunner, the rattlesnake cut into eighteen pieces by a grinning, stupid child. Legs of the iguana glow red on the plate, its three-foot skeleton smelling like the river, water forming jail cells of silt in the throats of those who never made it across. One survivor becomes the fingertip inside a cave telling the story of his belly button, his muted jaw, his back sweating against windows that open onto a concrete vault of flowers. This is how we regain bread inside cold ovens, stagger in four directions when there are five—the fifth mistaken for a burning piece of paper confiscated when the border was closed.

Why do we have to talk about another book? Why do we hold the squares of light as if they are tombstones given to us in a dance of time–silly fissures of anger and lust where the daily rushes of flowers opened to invite our eyes? Why do we have to tear the paragraph in two? Why does the sound of the waterfall echo as if we have never been there, drowning in the stove of black brick where the worst nightmare is only a dishonest shoulder, a version of the moon where we never return to answer the long legged kisses of strangers? Why do we have to turn the page? Why is the bookmark in a different place than last night, when the ribs separated and the dancer emerged in the fire? This plot is understood, the spine glued again into the volume before the sheets spill out and the pleasure is so great, we think we are dead.

He is extended singing. Let him in. Believe in his wish after his silence turns into scattered rugs on the floor of the mind. "What?" you ask. "Where?" How did his turtle make it to shore? When you raise your hands to feel for a pulse, do not hesitate. Plunge your arm all the way into the chest until you reach the greenhouse of the heart. When you pull out, say a prayer that doesn't lie, as something moves across the earth and he teaches you how to breathe. After all, the thunder you heard when you touched your belly button had nothing to do with the day you were born.

Part Four

Hot coffee in spite of beauty. A wish gaining momentum inside the month of the dragon, the day immersed in pollution thought to have become extinct by now. Corn dogs despised in the air, impregnated by a long sentence that got away from its misery, turned its letters on its author to wrap itself around the mouth of the devourer. Castle keeper. Blue pavilion. Orange skates exhibited as the last engines before water was invented. Pit bulls flaking skin on the street, challenging the dogcatcher to find religion before the cat scratches on his wrist are mistaken for maps pointing to where the dog bones are buried. Cease and desist. Turn the edges of the jukebox into three dozen tourists, their trip to the Atomic Museum rewarded with mushroom cloud t-shirts and a wind-up toy of Einstein mooning the world. Hot mammals on the lawn of the pigeons, the seeds arranged to tell a story, the momentum picking up strangers with terrorist conditions, frogs tied to firecrackers by nasty little boys wanting to be noticed, then given the pocket change from their parent's motel bill on swinging group night. Hot underlining discovered before it is too late, its erasure overseen by kings with technological damage. Their bowling balls are tucked away in basements overflowing with high school yearbooks that predicted these warriors would learn to read before globes of the earth were spun by their kids tired of throwing pennies at the animal control van.

In Memoriam

There is no one hiding under the leaves and the yard has been painted the wrong color. This practice was outlawed after the towers came down. The pause in breath demands meanings into the word—durations of rapture intended to sound the horn between the ears. Rusted frames of old cars and condemned houses rose out of the ground. Families moved back, regained their memories, and installed sensors in the bird feeders. This gave the vowels a chance to regain the strength they lost in the centuries of silence when few of us could follow the moving mouth toward something shared, then retold. There is no one giving water to the birds. This idea was accepted before the streets were paved, the pronouncement waiting for the end of the tale to jockey for position in the dusty books hidden on shelves. Tired widows and angry sons walked up and down the block, searching for lost dogs, pet canaries, and adopted children that ran away from home. There is no one witnessing the turning of the leaves because they are afraid to hold the weight of sentences that won't change the color of the brittle shapes. This desire was encouraged before the lights went out and the red and yellow flashes of fall were the moments when tiny breastbones were opened by an evolution so powerful, we forgot to take notes.

It occurs to me that the wheel entertains illicit love. It spins beyond flesh and image to sense how often I am able to avoid the hallway where the old man entered the room. A small white stone waited for him, but I took it that morning and ran across the street. This confession is troubled with moss covered cliffs—a touch of pink and the widest shore waiting for the old man to wipe his hands clean and leave the world. A smooth, polished jaw of a cat waits for me in the other house. When I break in, the bone glistens on the kitchen table, the dishes washed, the meal long gone. It might be wise to think of this before I go—once, I was that cat but now, my amphibious pose is enough to paint the walls green, hold back the sea until the old man sinks to the bottom of the ocean floor.

A.D.

The new dimension is a throat surviving the cost of stepping into the new style of century—outside settings tell us no one was kicked out of the calendar. Even the Aztecs lay down their tools and stared at the great stone wheels when they rolled out of the picture—the new dimension spits into the wind, carries a snap of rabbit and the lone commission found in the pocket of the king—how you carry this dilemma, its alternatives soaking in sunlight, leaving the small junction clean whistle setting the house down, until it implodes into the kneeling saint you have avoided since the pockets fell out of the river—a new dimension beats the clouds in asking for a chance to begin something—even a dish at the edge of the canyon was enough for eight Anazasi skeletons to finally disintegrate after seven hundred years—the opening in the plot means the stance will no longer do—deposits against planning, deposits against the body—when this new dimension is laughed at, laughing pleases the evidence and settles it beyond the house, beyond the trees where destruction is everything—screened to be aloof—a path inside the mountain more valuable than this—your lowered head healing and letting the horns lead the way into the rocks.

Cast motion out of the vesper dangling down to the vine pulled against wild choice retribution escape awareness of toy guest hallway system derived from lying to the dog unusual beauty causing the itch in the saddle that reached the installation first. Broken ribs broken man broken woman broken boy inside the thumb. Can the hoof prosper? Did the lettuce hanging from the bell feed the injured child? Did the rain fall as if the world had ended? Decide if the corner where you live belongs. Desperate cut back into fish history approaching faster than bleeding desire found years ago hidden from copulating marbles when you believed in the animal that blessed you missed you when it was time to steal four fingers from the affronted man loving the morning after the four fingers rubbed in oil to spell. The morning taught you to look under each wet eye demanding you consider it for the throne of laughter positioned between the legs the calling myth when you ask to be given an explanation a risk a rabid bat a token bone of departed fissures.

It was the end of the century. Men with shaved heads. Men with shaved heads worshipping the stone. Men with shiny heads believing the gun was the stone. It was near the end of the calendar. Teaching how to listen to the mouth that kisses the coldest stone. Turning the page, a new country is occupied. Underlining a passage to question him, boundaries are set in the brain. It was after a long battle. Naked men with shaved heads. Some of them talking among themselves. Some of them knowing what happened to the stone.

round hive burning Juan symbols his drums escapes behind the crossfire black masks of brothers take him round hive hissing Juan delivers a prayer rises with no feet black thoughts of brothers save him round hive grows Juan slows his brain figure on the cross burns him red car approaches *toca* starts its own heart drums like death not a rosary but a heart brown faces of brothers stunned Juan finds his own arms two ways out flees towards his father owner of the sin and the car *toca* beats like a hum cross made from medallions torn off sustained brothers Juan forcing his eyes open in time for the sirens to break the floor break his mind baskets of sparrows metal high black wings of brothers protecting Juan from phantoms in his house knocking on his head forcing him out no shirt on brown shield of sweat chest cross on chain memorizing *toca* memorizing communion regretting nothing Juan *toca* Juan of the face Juan of the father.

No knowledge without secrets they told him misbehaved in front of him did not let him see how the caraganda grew into a hairy shape inflicted harm by describing solid invasion without having to show him the tears of Saint Ignatius who was slain his head cut off his body picking it up walking with it to the spot where he wanted to be buried how this implies there is someone out there having been stolen from a slick kind of greed no system proclaimed with white engines buzzing inside familiar ghosts even wheels building new roads to protect the old roads styles coming back where the fire ants take over the yard burn themselves into a new stream odd even black as the vein that kept him alive with fresh ideas emerging from the humidity of the southern life insisting someone tell him how the books are always open to the right page who will read it to him before getting tired and hungry before the lights are turned out becoming turtles alive in the grass that heal without hesitation no knowledge with open equations satisfying the word the lords losing the ability to explain themselves even the reason for placing this part of their claws into the correct passage that will give us something to gain an idea swimming toward apprenticeship and the final start of a bright punctual edge held high over the heart.

When she came back, he was surprised—even the huge wings of the eagle in the painting stared at him. When he found the magnificent drawing of the panda bear, he saw something in its deep, black eyes—waiting for her to say something about the past, as if the brown woman in the blue waves explored his need to forgive. He surrounded himself with hundreds of postcards, paintings, drawings for a world that could curse no one like him—black bull with red stars, black horns above its white face, red stars snorting their way into his path. He found it where they sold the portrait of a wounded Kahlo, her naked sister dying in her bare lap, tentacles of green pleasure removing the sky around them. Frida's system was designed for his eyes and loneliness—her need to return filling him with an attraction for objects left on a spider web—a cat flying down the stairs—a black man embracing his trumpet as lights exploded off his leopard skin coat. The largest fragments of his sky became the water between continents as he dreamed the strawberry's seeds planted themselves in his ear—a manner of welcoming her back with a stomach that proclaimed love when she saw him and the seeds were swallowed to save him.

The Flash

It hits your vision like the needles in the air that survived the explosion in the desert, the mushroom cloud exposing history as starvation marches across the horizon, great metals of radioactive composers plunging through the other side. Being photographed takes patience like the young man crawling out of the river barely alive, barbed wire on the border recording his illegal secrets as number 8,539 for the month. The flash and you are the camera, the moment it happened the second you moved and someone who wasn't there appeared behind you in the print. When it was examined, the white shape was your great-great grandmother, dead forty-five years, waving one hand over your head, her gaping mouth the silent scream you were warned about when you were baptized as a child.

Man with Blue Guitar

Picasso painting

Bending down to pick up a piece of paper, I hear a sound coming out of my ears. Looking up, the skin glows as if I am wrong and the day will settle its differences, bring its strings to me. Straight and quiet, the wood is carved until the unknown friend holds it. I am alive to see this. When the chord is invented, I move over, let him sit next to me. He has something on his face. His fingers cannot be seen. There is no blue moment to define. It is entirely arranged to sound as if a day has opened and I have been let in. And it is always a burned blue city I find inside the tiny flask in my hands.

In the twinkling of an eye, the grazing donkey disappears, replaced by the drama of horses that are more in tune to the apocalypse. In the bending of the knee, youth is replaced by a flock of eagles sitting on a tall, dead cottonwood, the weight of the roosting birds about to topple its huge, gray trunk. In the twisted shape of the sculpture, the naked man is fired because they decide a costumed priest is better able to pray over the dead, his bible still smoldering. In the beating of the heart, the sea monster crawls onto the beach, massive waves washing over its proud body, the foam removing the blindfold from a woman who stands there waiting. In the prone position of sleep, rainbows appear on bedroom mirrors and wake the couple that had abandoned each other years ago. In the radio of electronic dreams, a caravan of giant toads sings about the end of the world but no one listens because their guitars are not plugged in. In the folded newspapers of one year, a politician pronounces that he believes in God while his staff dies from anthrax in hospitals. In the twinkling of an eye, the donkey returns, having survived the horses that out-raced the pieces of burning metal to the rising sun. In silhouette against the starving sun, the donkey keeps grazing, its desire to begin days of fasting broken by the greenest fields this side of the eclipse.

A man telling a stray dog to go home. A woman bending close to the sink, the diamond ring having disappeared down the drain. A man pointing to an indifferent cat to go lie down in the corner. A boy listening to footsteps upstairs. A girl hiding something in her dresser drawer before turning off the lights. A trumpet player painting his face red to disorient the spotlight on stage. A grandfather insisting he never tore the pages with the family tree out of the bible. A man yelling to a stray dog to get away from him. A grandmother folding something in her dresser drawer before going downstairs. A woman dressing quickly before the man wakes up and discovers she is his wife's twin sister. A boy making noise upstairs. A man kicking a stray dog. A girl misplacing something in a drawer and staying in the room, unable to find it. A volunteer crossing thin ice to see if the snowmobile fell through with its rider. A stray dog biting a man savagely on the leg. A woman bending close to the sink, her dripping hair sending drops of water all over the floor. A boy peering through the keyhole, holding his breath at what he sees. A girl finding a different object in the drawer than the one she was looking for. A volunteer falling through thin ice, his body not recovered until the thaw of spring. A man warmly embracing a stray dog, petting it, and taking it home.

Taphead loves me and gives me solar ice cream with back road syrup. Taphead shares his guitar, the holy coils measuring the weight of his breath his wife stole when she ran off with the drummer. Taphead loves me when I play his CD, the last song recorded to be played in reverse, but I can't the way I forced my Beatle LPs to spin backward on the turntable, *Revolver* screeching the message, "Taphead Loves Me." Taphead does love me and shares his wealth with my children, feeds them lunar popsicles from a broken down motorcycle Che Guevara willed to him. Taphead comes and goes, adores the way I write about him, his burning fingers, his collection of guitar picks he melted into teardrops that dripped on my bare feet the day Taphead entered my computer CD burner in search of a new virus I was never warned about.

How many wipes of the skin does it take to say farewell to the chameleon and welcome the sore lump in the throat? The thought is remembered when desire goes into exile and the armpit hides a totally different way of perspiring. Only the lips on the trumpet— their black focus sending spirals of contemplation across the fields of fresh chili. The thought trying to connect the sweating forehead with a taste for what burns on the mouthpiece of the horn. When this is accomplished, a thick pink candle draws near. As if the taken vowel is commissioned to be passionate, understanding, and open to seduction. A sweat to mark the maps, to wet the trail of anguish so there is no mistaking who is being loved and who is being cho-sen as the one to grieve.

Who carries the quiet shoulder in his lap? How can the new house diminish the city? Who has the right to the lizard hung in the cathedral? Which belief is rigid with fat bees humming in your hair? What did you say on the way to the lord juxtaposed in the ecstatic position of answering your prayers? What kind of bread did you eat? Who told you about drifting away from your heart and manner of reciting questions? Where did you go when the dead rose from the cemetery in the barrio, their dust the hair of eternity? Why do you insist the striking scorpion is the cure? Did you smell the iron spilling its elements in the soil you packed into your pockets? When will you choose the mask to wear when you admit it was restraint that broke the egg of the eagle soaring above your head for years, invisible beyond your answers? What happens to the wrinkled father you encountered after eight years? Why has he lost so much weight? When you share a meal with him, what happens to the food both of you swallow? Is it the passing of time or the end of nourishment?

So small beside the orange shadow of forgotten pipes withering among fallen hours when the outcast motion becomes a solid fold in the ancient hollow of a cornered and blackened claim to be seen without hurry counted among doubt the way of maintaining the quiet guitar perched on the burning logs fumigating earned rhythms as if this session was burned to bring Hendrix back reform his eyes to adjust to the madness of the electric world bring this favor upon the rolling whistle of a bird not listed in the book of birds fences and gates swallowed by mistake and the desire to be the first to discover the earthquake why does someone believe the monument behaves sits down to phantom and commission a small tower hungry for wise eyes this rock this hole a prism for the forest and the kissed paper in ink without reason or form or the branded sound of the log guitar breaking into three stars broken chairs sit at the end of the story as if each man holds a cane and glass of juice to be forgotten replenished as a young traveler that went to the wrong country made love to an old woman who left him defeated and dry with every movement of body and fissure a man in his forties pressing his body into the shape of the twig and the caterpillar whose long black hair turns orange when he wakes from the mystery that left him to gather each feather that fell through the open window each naked breast resembling a globe of light that taught him to be the first child.

When you laugh to laugh, it is a sign of love from a Dali painting where bodies come apart to reinvent a story of love. When you choose to be quiet, it is a beautiful ballet, your legs caressing the clouds. When you ruby for grief, the rubbing is a sadness that ends the night with a swollen dream where the horses arrive in time to bring you dust. When you quote from stones you found in a bird's nest, no one believes you. You hold onto their abstract thoughts like—"Take that ladybug out of my eye," or "Look at the weasel climbing his back," then, "What if I touch his dahlia? Will it grow through my third arm?" When you laugh to laugh, you are instructed in the fine art of love. When you wake in a small room, turn in the darkness and say what you have never said, "Please, listen. The time of the crusades is near."

WHAT COLOR IS YOUR MEXICAN?

I have folded the ancestral cross, quit praying so someone can believe me. In the photo, Pancho Villa hangs out the door of his bullet-riddled car, the assassins fleeing across the bridge. There is an electric guitar that won't die, Emilio Zapata's sombrero dominating the tourist shop poster, statues of turquoise coyotes selling faster than guns. I have a postcard of Frida Kahlo exposing her breasts to a bird while Diego makes love to her sister in the other room, this vision making me show my friends the falcon on my arm, how its hood falls when I stop to catch my breath. Octavio Paz finally meets my dead grandmother, their whispering in the great mansion turning my hair gray, this dream coming three weeks after her funeral. I have a statue of a Spanish conquistador, sword drawn to repel what anyone thinks, Edward Curtis invading the Hopi by capturing the snake dance before his camera shattered on the rocks. I think about the woman with the swollen flowers in her ears, how she admitted the saxophone of her lover was more important than being able to cry, Bob Dylan angry in the documentary, throwing cue cards at the camera, walking off with a grin. I hear the band warming up, the drums hesitating, my lyrics to be sung to a sweating, angry crowd, Mick Jagger mesmerized by the Hell's Angels stabbing the black dude at Altamont. The color of my skin turns brown when the border is closed, white when I burn my words into the books, my body intercepting the future until Hernan Cortes gives up the Aztec gold, Subcomandante Marcos rips off his black Zapatista mask, and I steal a bowl of arrowheads, one shattering on the glass table, its green eye as dark as the bats flying out of the caverns, covering the desert with what can never come out.

What happened when the sparrow went down? Ghost snow mocked my eyes and the wind moved toward dying. I repeated the moaning of the surge—an afternoon dismantled of sound, its quiet god missing his ability to skin the horizon of its color, steal from the scrolling of time. I miss the king, too, but have been startled too often by cooing doves. What gift was taken when the bird punctured the office tower, left its seeds scattered across carpeted floors, the history of someone else's body? There must be something wrong because the sky is full of objects and the windmill is on fire, forcing me to scratch with the infinite claw of a bloodthirsty one hundred years. Once I had an acoustic guitar with only five strings—to charge me with this responsibility would be like commanding me not to sleep as I wait for the millennium butterfly to rumple my hair with a black gloved, closed fist. I was taken there by a monk who believed in broken treaties, a silly, silent man who hated the way I crossed the water without looking back. This must be true. He no longer stands here, now replaced by balconies that are no longer islands. The snow blew and out of the corner of my eye, I counted fourteen pleasures, including the one where we are dark creatures whispering under the bed. Even this has possibilities when I stalk the blowing newspaper on the sidewalk, stepping on it before the headlines change. I don't know what to do. The final time I saw my first grade teacher, she was flying through the air with her hair on fire. She saw me, screamed without a sound, her comet arcing over the earth to hold me on the playground, make me go to the reading circle full of dummies who could barely read, the fact I was smarter than all of them hidden by the wall of Spanish I threw at them, the teacher punishing me, crashing like the bomb someone planted to disrupt the day, force the students to run for home before their perfect English could save them from the explosion that has not ceased to this day. To give you that memory is to report for duty inside the tree, but I've hesitated in asking you to wake in a holy place, count your blessings and give me an angel, a skull or two. I don't want the shield or the tape recorder, only the vinyl LP music that is harder than the omens of death. I have enough Hendrix videos. The CD institutions have been notified of this, while half my arm is submerged in the cactus—glow deep thorn fused against traffic, corn based sombrero thief stereotyped coughing bandit. When I return, I will see the grass in the backyard turn yellow and I will live in the lap of a mountain. There are no houses there, only shelves of rifles locked in vaults my angry children left there, something to start a conversation when my calendar runs out of days and its grass turns greener than what goes out and never returns. When you decide about this, or why the sparrow went down, don't bother it. Its wings are folded and it's already sleeping inside my shoes.

The Bird of Dreams

It was huge and hovered mightily, with a blue and red head. I couldn't see its wings, thought of a giant hummingbird. This bird came out of the gray sun to trace the lines on the face of a strange god before flying into view, suspended over me, letting me know the sun would turn back to yellow upon the tapping of the bell, the start of the music, the moment I opened my eyes to see the wing of color was the extended arm I was told about before I was born.

Ray Gonzalez is the author of *Turtle Pictures* (Arizona, 2000), which received the 2001 Minnesota Book Award for Poetry, and a collection of essays, *The Underground Heart: A Return to a Hidden Landscape* (Arizona, 2002), which received the 2003 Texas Institute of Letters Award for Best Book of Non-fiction. He is the author of nine books of poetry, including four from BOA Editions—*The Heat of Arrivals* (1997 PEN/Oakland Josephine Miles Book Award), *Cabato Sentora, The Hawk Temple at Tierra Grande* (2003 Minnesota Book Award for Poetry and a National Book Critic's Circle Award Notable Book Citation), and the forthcoming *Consideration of the Guitar: New and Selected Poems*. He is the author of two collections of short stories, *The Ghost of John Wayne* (Arizona, 2001, winner of a 2002 Western Heritage Award for Short Fiction) and *Circling the Tortilla Dragon* (Creative Arts, 2002). His poetry has appeared in the 1999, 2000, and 2003 editions of *The Best American Poetry* (Scribners) and *The Pushcart Prize: Best of the Small Presses 2000* (Pushcart Press). He is the editor of twelve anthologies, most recently *No Boundaries: Prose Poems by 24 American Poets* (Tupelo Press, 2002). He has served as Poetry Editor of The Bloomsbury Review for twenty-three years and founded LUNA, a poetry journal, in 1998. He is Full Professor in the MFA Creative Writing Program at The University of Minnesota in Minneapolis.